IMAGES OF WAR

FALLSCHIRMJÄGER: GERMAN PARATROOPERS 1937–1941

IMAGES OF WAR

FALLSCHIRMJÄGER: GERMAN PARATROOPERS 1937–1941

RARE PHOTOGRAPHS FROM WARTIME ARCHIVES

FRANÇOIS COCHET

Pen & Sword
MILITARY

AN IMPRINT OF PEN & SWORD BOOKS LTD.
YORKSHIRE - PHILADELPHIA

Originally published in 2009 by Editions de Krijger as *Fallschirmjäger: Les Parachutistes Allemands (Tome I: 1937-1941)*

First published in Great Britain in 2019 by
Pen & Sword Military
An imprint of
Pen & Sword Books Ltd
Yorkshire - Philadelphia

Copyright © François Cochet, 2019

ISBN 978 1 52674 066 3

Typeset in 12/14.5 Gill Sans by Aura Technology and Software Services, India
Printed and bound in India by Replika Press Pvt Ltd.

Pen & Sword Books Ltd incorporates the Imprints of Pen & Sword Books Archaeology, Atlas, Aviation, Battleground, Discovery, Family History, History, Maritime, Military, Naval, Politics, Railways, Select, Transport, True Crime, Fiction, Frontline Books, Leo Cooper, Praetorian Press, Seaforth Publishing, Wharncliffe and White Owl.

For a complete list of Pen & Sword titles please contact

PEN & SWORD BOOKS LIMITED
47 Church Street, Barnsley, South Yorkshire, S70 2AS, England
E-mail: enquiries@pen-and-sword.co.uk
Website: www.pen-and-sword.co.uk

or
PEN AND SWORD BOOKS
1950 Lawrence Rd, Havertown, PA 19083, USA
E-mail: uspen-and-sword@casematepublishers.com
Website: www.penandswordbooks.com

Contents

Introduction

The bloody fighting of the German *Fallschirmjäger* (paratroopers) of the Second World War had inspired many kinds of books due to the fact that, assimilated to elite troops, airborne units of the Third Reich were regularly engaged at the forefront of the fighting. Famous victories, including the raid on the Belgian fort of Eben-Emael in May 1940 and the battles for control of the big island of Crete just a year later, remained in the collective unconscious, granting the paratroopers a kind of aura (sometimes a little exaggerated) and building an excellent esprit de corps amongst the troops.

In any case, however, the 'great age' of the *Fallschirmtruppen* (parachute units) was to end in 1941. From 1942 until the end of the conflict, German paratroopers were most often deployed in a more 'classical' way, although some battles (like Cassino or Leros) allowed them to reconnect with their recent and glorious past.

Image Credits - The majority of photographs in this book are from the author's collection, as well as those of several other people: Bernd Bosshammer, Jean-Pierre Chantrain, Jean-Louis Roba and Peter Taghon. Documents also come from *Der Adler* magazine and from various contemporary books on the *Fallschirmjäger*. Thanks must go to all those who helped to make this book.

Mini Glossary

ANZAC: Australian and New Zealand troops.

Barbarossa: German code name for the invasion of the USSR on 22 June 1941.

Blitzkrieg: lightning war.

Der Adler: 'The Eagle' (the official illustrated Luftwaffe magazine).

DFS 230: German transport glider.

Enigma: German encoded transmission machine.

Fall Gelb: Plan Yellow (German code name for the invasion of Western Europe on 10 May 1940).

Fallschirmjäger: German paratrooper.

Festung Holland: 'Fortress Netherlands'

FJR: Parachute Regiment (*Fallschirmjägerregiment*).

Fliegerdivision: German Air Division.

Fliegerkorps: German air corps.

Feldwebel: colour sergeant.

Generalmajor: Major General.

Heer: German army.

Heldenfriedhof: literally ''heroes' cemetery'', a German military cemetery.

Hauptmann: captain.

Infanteriedivision: infantry division.

Ju 52: German three-engine transport aircraft manufactured by Junkers.

Leutnant: second lieutenant.

Luftwaffe: German air force

Marita: German code name for the invasion of Greece.

Merkur: German code name for the invasion of Crete.

MG: machine gun (*Maschinengewehr*).

Oberleutnant: first lieutenant.

Oberst: colonel.

RAD: Reich Labour Service (*Reichsabeitsdienst*).

RAF: British Air Force (Royal Air Force).

Rekrutenzeit: training period for a military recruit.

Ritterkreuz: Knight's Cross of the Iron Cross.

Ritterkreuzträger (or RKT): a recipient of the *Ritterkreuz*.

Seelöwe: Sea lion (German code name for the invasion of England).

Sturmregiment: assault regiment (one of the German airborne units).

Ultra: British apparatus decrypting Enigma messages.

Unternehmen: operation.

Wehrmacht: the unified armed forces of Germany - aviation (*Luftwaffe*), army (*Heer*) and navy (*Kriegsmarine*).

Weserübung: German code name for the invasion of Scandinavia.

Useful dates for this volume

11 November 1918: end of the First World War.

28 June 1919: Treaty of Versailles.

16 April 1922: Treaty of Rapallo aimed at a rapprochement between Germany and the USSR.

30 January 1933: Adolf Hitler is appointed as Chancellor of the Reich and the Nazi Party take overall power of the German government.

15 May 1933: Ministry of Aviation (*Reichsluftfahrtministerium*) is established.

29 January 1936: first *Fallschirmjäger* units are established.

1 July 1938: *Generalmajor* Kurt Student takes command of German airborne units.

23 August 1939: Nazi-Soviet Pact.

1 September 1939: German troops invade Poland.

3 September 1939: Great Britain and France declare war on Germany. Beginning of the Second World War.

17 September 1939: Soviet troops invade Poland. Polish government leaves for Romania.

26 September 1939: end of the Polish campaign.

7 April 1940: start of Operation *Weserübung* (German invasion of Denmark and Norway).

13 April 1940: Second Battle of Narvik.

14 April 1940: Allies land at Narvik and Namsos.

1 May 1940: surrender of Norwegian troops.

5 May 1940: the king of Norway and his government leave for London.

10 May 1940: start of the *Westfeldzug*. Capture of Eben-Emael and the bridges on the Albert Canal.

German paratroopers jump into the Netherlands.

13 May 1940: Allied attacks on Narvik.

14 May 1940: bombing of Rotterdam.

15 May 1940: surrender of the Netherlands army.

3 June 1940: Retreat of Allied troops in Norway.

4 June 1940: fall of Dunkirk.

21 June 1940: the French surrender is signed in Rethondes.

16 July 1940: Hitler issues *Kriegsweisung* No. 16, authorising Operation *Seelöwe* (the invasion of Great Britain).

13 August 1940: start of the major German aerial offensives on England.

28 October 1940: Adolf Hitler meets Benito Mussolini in Florence following the launch of the Italian offensive against Greece. The Führer does not offer to send *Fallschirmjäger*.

29 October 1940: Commonwealth troops land on the island of Crete.

10 December 1940: transfer of X. *Fliegerkorps* to Sicily. Germany is now committed in the Mediterranean.

11 December 1940: Operation Felix (capture of Gibraltar) officially abandonned.

13 December 1940: Hitler issues *Kriegsweisung* No. 20, authorising Operation Marita (the invasion of Greece).

18 December 1940: Hitler issues *Kriegsweisung* No. 21, authorising Operation Barbarossa (the invasion of the USSR).

11 January 1941: Hitler issues *Kriegsweisung* No. 22, authorising the engagement of German units in the Mediterranean.

8 February 1941: Great Britain agrees to provide military support to Greece.

12 February 1941: General Erwin Rommel arrives in Tripoli.

14 March 1941: end of the Italian offensive in Albania.

24 March 1941: beginning of General Rommel's counter-offensive in Africa.

27 March 1941: drafting of *Kriegsweisung* No. 25 - the attack on Yugoslavia.

6 April 1941: start of Operation *Marita* (the invasion of Greece and Yugoslavia).

25 April 1941: Hitler issues *Kriegsweisung* No. 26, Operation *Merkur* (the invasion of Crete).

26 April 1941: Battle of the Corinth Canal.

27 April 1941: fall of Athens.

30 April 1941: Hitler sets the launch of Operation *Barbarossa* to 22 June.

10 May 1941: Rudolf Hess flies to Scotland.

20 May 1941: Operation *Merkur* is launched.

21 May 1941: capture of Maleme aerodrome. German fleets bringing reinforcements is pushed back by the Royal Navy.

24 May 1941: German radio officially announces for the first time that they are fighting in Crete.

25 May 1941: heavy fighting in Galatas.

26 May 1941: Germans capture Galatas.

27 May 1941: Order given to evacuate Crete. Chania falls into German hands.

28 May 1941: the airborne capture Souda Bay.

29 May 1941: fall of Heraklion and Rethymnon

2 June 1941: end of Operation *Merkur*. Crete is now entirely in the hands of the Axis Forces.

22 June 1941: launch of Operation *Barbarossa* (invasion of the USSR).

17 July 1941: Hitler meets with generals Kurt Student and Julius Ringel, the 'Victors of Crete'.

19 July 1941: drafting of *Kriegsweisung* No. 33, authorising the continuation of the war in the East.

21 August 1941: Hitler orders the capture of Crimea, and the encirclements of Kiev and Leningrad.

2 October 1941: Operation *Taifun* (Typhoon) - the German advance towards Moscow. Hitler addresses those men fighting on the Eastern Front.

9 October 1941: Hitler officially announces that the USSR has been defeated.

11 December 1941: Italy and Germany declare war on the USA.

20 December 1941: withdrawal of German troops in the East to their winter positions.

Chapter 1

The Origins of the *Fallschirmtruppen*

The Great War 1914-18 had hardly seen the use of paratroopers. Almost until the very end of the conflict, few airmen had made use of this vital weapon; hence the high rate of losses in their ranks.

The first offensive units (paratroopers) equipped with parachutes were actually first used by the Soviets around 1928. Pushed aside at the time by the democracies, the USSR was innovative in all areas in order to make room for "class enemies". Weimar Germany, annihilated and degraded by the famous Treaty of Versailles in 1919, was only authorised to maintain a standing army of 100,000 men. Its leaders were forced, by necessity, to keep abreast of any novelty in military matters. Having become an objective ally of Bolshevik Russia thanks to the rapprochement of the two 'plague victims', the Weimar Republic decided to train its airmen on the Soviet base at Lipeztk, in the greatest secrecy. Exchanges of technique and skill became commonplace and allowed German specialists to quickly learn about the importance of paratroopers. When cooperation between the Soviet Union and Germany ended after 1933 (when the National Socialists came to power in Germany), this new weapon found its place in a rapidly expanding Luftwaffe. Contrary to popular beliefs imposed after 1945, but still taken for granted by some 'scholars', Hitler did not create the *Wehrmacht* with a magic wand, but benefited greatly from earlier efforts by the military leaders of the Weimar Republic. However, it would take around three years to put this project on track. On 29 January 1936, the German Air Ministry ordered the transfer of several volunteers from the '*Regiment General Göring*' (former Prussian police group) to a school to serve as parachute instructors. The school itself was initially located in Neubrandenburg, before moving to Stendal.

After various trial and errors, the command of the airborne troops was entrusted to a veteran, General Kurt Student. Born on 12 May 1890 in Brandenburg, the Student had entered the *Reichswehr* around 1911, but had quickly left for the nascent aviation branch of the military. In the first weeks of the Great War, Student was assigned to FFA 17, which was operating in the East, where he won his first victory. In 1915 he was transferred to units on the Western Front and commanded *Jasta*

9 in 1916. Wounded in action in 1917, he ended the war with six air victories to his credit. Although paradoxically he remained in the new German army after the defeat in 1918, when all military aviation was prohibited in the Weimar Republic, this aviation ace would be put to good use and was assigned to a section for 'technical development'. Student was one of many (including in the USSR) who was furious at the situation and was ready to prepare for the revival of his country's military aviation abilities. This would take place on 1 September 1933, when this highly qualified lieutenant colonel was called to the newly created Air Ministry (*Reichsluftministerium*). Initially in command of the Rechlin training centre, Student made contact with the paratroopers once he became Schools Inspector. On 1 July 1938, the former Great War ace took effective command of the new *7. Flieger (Fallschirm-) Division*, which gathered together the various parachute regiments that existed at the time. His name and destiny would now be forever linked to the *Fallschirmtruppen*.

The coming to power of the National Socialists would pave the way for the rebirth of the German armed forces (land, air and navy) and thus push many young people to join the military. To begin with unemployment was a certainty for many, but as the years passed, volunteers were mainly attracted by the prestige surrounding airmen, paratroopers or crews of submarines, who were all considered to be "*Draufganger*" (go-getters).

Under the Third Reich, every young man had to complete an obligatory six-month internship at the RAD (the *Reichsarbeitsdienst* or labour service) to complete work that could be seen as being 'of general interest'. During subsequent military service, he could choose one of the three branches of the armed forces. Volunteers and reservists had first to undergo the *Rekrutenzeit*, the period when recruits devoted their time to learning the basics of military life (receiving their uniform, discipline, marches and various exercises, etc.). This period lasted around eight weeks, at the end of which tests were used to estimate the capabilities of the new soldier and allocate him into a unit.

Physical prowess was certainly essential to becoming a paratrooper. On the other hand, contrary to what some might say, not all paratroopers were volunteers. According to one former *Fallschirmjäger*:

I was waiting in a room with another soldier. We had to choose a branch of the Luftwaffe, but we hesitated. Flying staff? Communications? It was then that an officer entered the room. It was [Hermann-Bernhard] Ramcke, but we didn't know him yet. He stared at us and said, "You two will make good paratroopers. Follow me!" We didn't object and automatically stood up and left the room right behind him. That's how we became paratroopers!

In addition to these rather unusual cases, the airborne troops would inherit young volunteers who had initially made another choice (such as the flying staff), but who failed the very specific training. Rather than become ground crew again, the disappointed aviators preferred instead to swell the ranks of the *Fallschirmjäger*.

The morale of German airborne troops originated in the training given to the students. From the start, the future parachutist had to know his equipment back to front. He had to fold his own parachute, which forced him to check its condition continuously. According to an old paratrooper, 'Each of us was responsible for his own life. We folded our parachutes ourselves. The delivery of a parachute that had already been prepared was the harbinger of a special mission.'

After studying the equipment, the aspiring young parachutist would be subjected to intense physical training. He first had to 'jump' in the room before being introduced to his machine, the three-engined Junkers 52/3m, from which he would jump. He had to learn to land safely before recovering the heavy weapon that had been parachuted nearby, most often in containers. When the group was considered ready, it boarded a Ju 52 to make its first proper jump. The student had to learn to hang the rope that would open his parachute properly, as well as automatically. Because the time spent in the air had to be as short as possible, the jumps took place between 120 and 200 metres, which precluded the use of a manual parachute. Each *Fallschirmjäger* tied a rope to a rail and jumped without worrying about the rest. After guiding his fall, the paratrooper had to make sure not to injure himself when he made contact with the ground, and not be dragged along by his parachute which sometimes got caught in strong winds. The course lasted eight weeks and included six jumps from a Ju 52. Accidents seem to have been quite rare, with the exception of a few crushed vertebrae and many sprained ankles. Pupils who did not pass this stage, either through fear or lack of physical ability, were then most often transferred to Luftwaffe ground crew units. Success in the training allowed him to receive the parachutist's metal badge (a diving eagle), before being assigned to a regiment where the training would be pushed to the maximum. The young *Fallschirmjäger* would learn how to be thrown into the heat of a battle, recover his weapons as quickly as possible and then regroup with his comrades to face the enemy.

General Kurt Student, whose name would remain inextricably linked to the German paratroopers of the Third Reich. Note that he is wearing the badge of ex-members of the Imperial German Flying Corps. Student was, indeed, a fighter pilot during the First World War.

Between 1933 and 1944, every young German was required to carry out various forms of heavy duty work for the benefit of the community, as part of the RAD (Reich Labour Service).

After six months service with the RAD, the militiaman could apply for his weapon. Upon entering the unit (in this case the Luftwaffe), an oath-taking ceremony was held over the flag, as was done in all armies at the time.

The oath was repeated by the recruits, now in formation.

During the *Rekrutenzeit* (training period), forced marches were one of the many obligations of the future soldier. As the German military would say, "*Schweiss spart Blut*" (sweat spares blood).

The young men who had opted for the paratroopers were then sent to Stendal or Wittstock to receive special training. The indoor jump was the first exercise undertaken by all *Fallschirmjäger* candidates.

A positional exercise, still in the classroom. When jumping at low altitude, the *Fallschirmjäger* had to adopt a suitable position in order to land safely.

Each paratrooper was responsible for folding his own parachute.

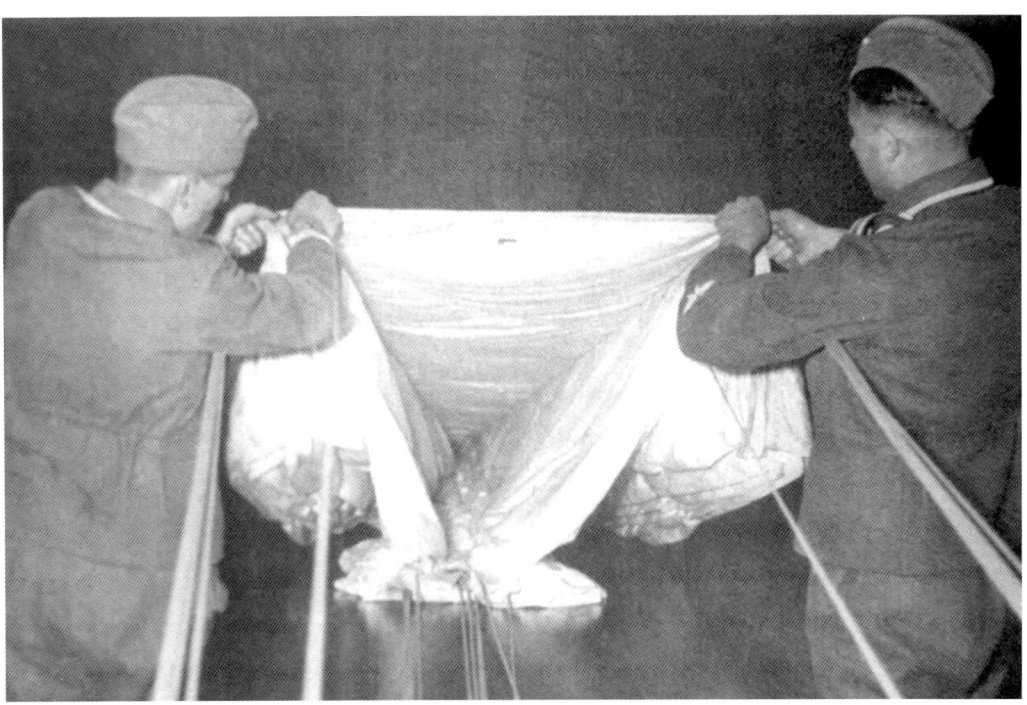

The folding of the parachute was certainly a tiresome, but nevertheless vital, operation.

After the indoor exercises, the future paratrooper learned to roll on the ground to lessen the impact.

The men also had to learn how to fall correctly....

... even when wearing the typical *Fallschirmjäger* helmet.

In peacetime, the paratrooper must recover the precious silk from his parachute. Out in the field, an instructor explains how to do this.

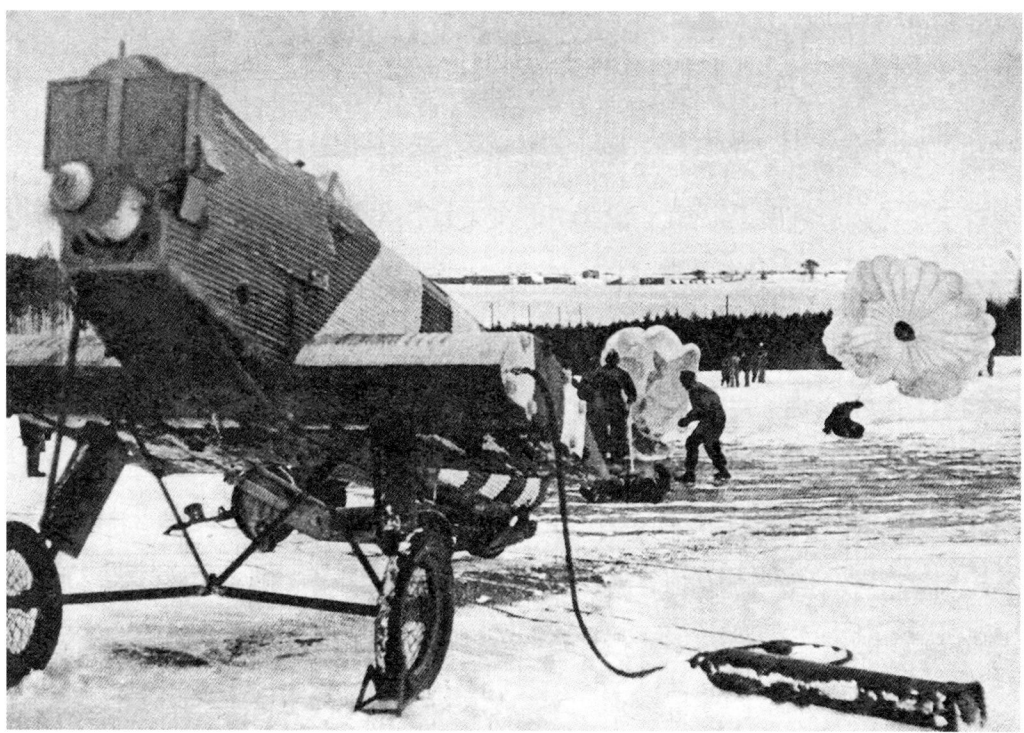

To learn how to combat strong winds, the future paratroopers are tied to a 'Windesel', an old and specially adapted aeroplane whose wings have been removed.

A more 'modern' Hs 126, devoid of its parasol wing, also serves as a 'Windesel'.

To give an idea of the narrowness of the Ju 52's door through which the paratroopers had to jump, exercises also took place with a three-engine plane on the ground.

The big moment has arrived: an instructor checks that the parachute is in its proper place.

The students are encased in the Ju 52's narrow fuselage. In the training school, the aircraft could carry twelve students (plus the three crewmen) with their equipment, a jump monitor and a supervisor.

The first jump for a group of young recruits from Wittstock training school. Some of their faces look a little tense...

A good jump, just like in training, but now you are no longer on the ground!

As soon as the paratrooper has jumped, the rope triggers the automatic opening of his parachute.

The descent is fast.

Fatal accidents were rare in training, but sprained ankles were not unusual...

As soon as the men touched the ground, they had to regroup as soon as possible. This paratrooper appears to have lost his helmet, which means this photograph was probably taken for propaganda purposes.

Fallschirmjäger in combat position after their jump. These more sophisticated training exercises took place in the units where the aspiring paratrooper had been paid after having obtained his basic certificate.

The recovery of a container filled with heavy weaponry. The *Fallschirmjäger* would jump with his pistol, at most.

Above: The *7.Fliegerdivision* included some small specialised units, such as these engineers.

Below: An MG 34 heavy machine gun under the curious eyes of a child from the nearby village.

Bruno Bräuer, one of the great figures among German paratroopers. Born in Berlin in 1893, he served as a non-commissioned officer during the First World War, where he was wounded. After becoming a police officer in Prussia, in 1933 he was one of the first members of the 'Hermann Göring' group before applying to the paratroopers, where he would eventually lead a battalion.

Deployed in the Netherlands in May 1940 and in Crete a year later, he would also fight on the Eastern Front. To his misfortune, in 1942 he was promoted to commander on Crete (*Festung Kreta*) which would force him to order or condone retaliations against the civilian population. In December 1944 he led the 9th Parachute Division, which was deployed in the defence of Breslau and Berlin.

In 1945, Bräuer was handed over to the Greek government, which, in the middle of a civil war, condemned him to death as an example to others, and executed him in 1947. In this picture, you can clearly see the metal badge of the German paratroopers (a diving eagle) below the harness.

Chapter 2

The Beginnings of the Second World War (Poland and Scandinavia)

In 1939, *7.Fliegerdivision* gathered together all of the paratroopers in its ranks. The previous year, the few *Fallschirmjäger* who were still attached somewhat anarchically to the *Heer* (army) were finally brought under this seventh air division. In addition to two parachute regiments, the division also had a heavy artillery battery, an anti-tank company, a medical unit and various other specialised detachments.

On 1 September 1939, the German army invaded Poland. In spite of the disproportionate hopes that France and Great Britain placed in the strength of the Polish army, it was broken in only a few days. The German advance was such that the airborne troops didn't even have time to be deployed. Objectives were laid out but, even before the paratroopers were told of their mission, the armoured advance had already captured those strategic points. In mid-September, however, part of the first paratrooper regiment was sent to occupy airfields between the Vistula and the Bug so as to defend them against those Polish units which had been cut off from the bulk of their troops. For the majority of troops this was a simple military exercise, but a serious engagement with Polish soldiers near Demblin would cost the lives of some of those *Fallschirmjäger* who were deployed there as mere infantrymen. Although the novelty of the *Blitzkrieg* (lightning war) delighted the military circles in Berlin, it was the source of much disappointment for the *Fallschirmjäger,* who were unable to take pride in the campaign, with certain paratroopers already thinking of transferring to other Luftwaffe units so they could see more action.

The Scandinavia campaign (Operation *Weserübung*) in April 1940 helped restore the new German paratrooper's tarnished coat of arms. Twenty-four hours before the Allied landed their forces, the *Wehrmacht* invaded Denmark and Norway, thus protecting the Swedish 'iron road'. This time, the parachutists found themselves at the forefront of the fighting as a result of the very long distances that needed to be covered. Thus, in the early morning of 9 April, the fourth company from FJR1 (1st paratrooper regiment) jumped from its aircraft over Denmark and, without a shot being fired, seized the Storstrøm bridge, which consequently allowed the ground troops to advance quickly to Copenhagen. At the same time, the Norwegian aerodrome at Stavanger-Sola was captured by the third company. Its capture involved Luftwaffe units and now made it possible to attack maritime objectives. On the other hand, the capture of Fornebu (Oslo aerodrome) failed due to a thick mist which obscured the objective and prevented any jump from taking place.

First company was to distinguish itself out in the snowy Norwegian expanses when its men parachuted near Dombas to prevent British and Norwegian forces from joining up. Although the drop wasn't successful, the airborne troops fought valiantly for four days before surrendering. Finally, towards the end of May, the *Fallschirmjäger* supported General Eduard Dietl's mountain troops who were in action in Narvik and gained a reputation as tenacious fighters.

However, as the Scandinavian campaign pushed on further north, the exploits of the airborne, although trumpeted by the propaganda of the Third Reich, always seemed to be somewhat mythical. It was not until the invasion of Western Europe that the German airborne would carve out its reputation, only a short distance from the borders of the Reich.

During the Polish campaign, paratroopers would be sent to hold recently captured airfields.

Above: Ju 52s arrive with *Fallschirmjäger* in Kielce. The airborne would hardly see any action against the Polish troops.

Below: The containers would stay wisely stored in the Ju 52s.

Some of the *Fallschirmjäger* crossed Poland by truck.

Taking a break in Poland.

Most of the time, the *Fallschirmjäger* would be content to look at the leftovers from the German victory, such as this PZL P-24 Polish fighter aircraft, which was found on an airfield.

The Norwegian campaign would restore the reputation of the airborne. Here, paratroopers are awaiting departure on the morning of 9 April 1940.

After the capture of several Scandinavian airfields, the paratroopers would be deployed in a more traditional way in Dombas and Narvik.

To Oslo.

Supplies also had to be be parachuted into these isolated areas.

Snow often softened the contact with the ground.

The fighting in the north was tough.

May 1940: Belgium and the Netherlands (Operation *Fall Gelb*)

Since their joint declaration of war on the Reich on 3 September 1939, the Franco-British allies had held the line on the other side of the Rhine. In 1940, however, it was time to break the military stalemate. The plan was Operation *Fall Gelb* (Case Yellow), a westward attack involving the invasion of three neutral countries (the Netherlands, Belgium and the Grand Duchy), which would then force the Franco-British troops to leave the French borders and venture north. They would then be surrounded and cut off from their rear guard following the rapid advance of a large and very mobile armoured formation through the Belgian Ardennes.

The German paratroopers, as special units, could not be deployed as mere infantrymen, and instead were instead tactically used to deceive the British. A large detachment was ordered to take control of the bridges on the Albert Canal at the Dutch-Belgian border (the waterway would otherwise pose a formidable obstacle for tanks). But, in order for the raid to be effective, it was also necessary to annihilate the Belgian fortress of Eben-Emael, considered by many to be 'impregnable'. The fort's guns, which covered the bridges, would only be able to hinder the progress of the two armoured divisions as they charged towards the centre of Belgium with the aim of attracting enemy troops. The task seemed impossible, but the *Fallschirmäger* would use a weapon that at the time was relatively unknown: the glider. Embarking in a DFS 230, the airborne troops would land either near the bridges or on the (undefended) banks of the fortress, and put the garrison out of action by using hollow, or shaped, charges, which again were relatively unknown, but devastating, weapons. The group specifically charged with taking the fort (the 'Concrete Group') had the opportunity to train extensively on Czech fortified positions, which were built on the same principles as Eben-Emael, and had fallen into German hands following the annexation of Czechoslovakia in 1939.

In the early hours of 10 May 1940, the Ju 52 drawing the DFS 230 gliders took off from aerodromes near the border and despite various hazards, the gliders landed near or on their objectives. The Belgian soldiers were surprised to see the arrival of these amazing aircraft, painted white and devoid of any marks of nationality. Although the defenders were able to blow up one bridge, the others fell, intact, into German hands and were taken over by the *Panzerdivisionen* after they had filled the area with anti-aircraft guns. Meanwhile, the Eben-Emael fort quickly surrendered after its garrison was disoriented by the invaders coming from the roof. The *Fallschirmjäger* thus entered history at the top of the ladder on 10 May 1940. Propaganda would often give them a somewhat disproportionate place in magazines and books, but it was at Eben-Emael that the legend of the 'invincible paratroopers' was born.

However, the Albert Canal was not all. Another much larger fortress, the 'Festung Holland', also had to be taken. The paratroopers were vigorously and effectively deployed in the Netherlands with the aim of paralysing the resistance of the local army by fragmenting its forces and undermining its communications. To do this, around 4,000 *Fallschirmjäger* had to be dropped in the heart of the country and take control of not only the aerodromes, but also key buildings and structures in order to ensure the rapid advance of the *Heer*'s troops. For this major operation to succeed, 585 Ju 52s were required and on the morning of 10 May 1940, this air armada crossed the Netherlands, heading for Rotterdam and The Hague. This time, Student's men would be supported by 12,000 soldiers from *22. Infanteriedivision* (22nd Infantry Division), who were also transported by three-engined aircraft. The planes were to land at various Dutch aerodromes, once they had been captured by the airborne troops, and deposit their cargo of infantry. But unlike the operation for the Albert Canal, in this instance the original plan couldn't be fully realised. There were not enough paratroopers for this important task, while the Dutch DCA was very active and shot down the Ju 52s with their passengers. Other aircraft, disoriented by such strong resistance, went off course and ended up dropping men everywhere. The royal family and the Dutch government managed to escape enemy capture and fled to Great Britain. Despite these mishaps, the capture of the Waalhaven aerodrome near Rotterdam allowed the 22. I.D. to be transported by air, leading to the capture of the strategic city. The Germans' control of the Moerdijk and Dordrecht bridges facilitated the advance of the land units as they rushed into the Netherlands and rescued the encircled airborne troops. After four days of fighting, the Dutch army surrendered. This success was largely due to the actions of the *Fallschirmjäger*. The speed of the German advance would, however, be misinterpreted by the British, who attributed the success to paratroopers disguised as nuns, priests or Dutch soldiers acting as a "fifth column". The need to land the Ju 52s to unload troops from the 22. I.D. made some strategists across the Channel believe that airborne troops had primarily to be landed in this way (and not dropped from the air). It would take more than a year for the British to assimilate the German tactics of employing *Fallschirmjäger*.

Ju 52s are gathered on the Karsch airfield on 9 May 1940, ready to take part in the attack on the Netherlands. The invasion of the West would begin the following day.

A group of paratroopers equipped for combat stand in front of a plane, ready to receive the last instructions from their platoon leader.

A paratrooper in battle dress.

One of the main objectives on 10 May 1940 was the Albert Canal, particularly its bridges and the Eben-Emael Fort. The canal effectively acted as a gigantic anti-tank ditch.

Above: In the weeks leading up to May, the paratroopers were able to train on the Czech fortifications that had fallen into German hands the previous year, and which were comparable to the Belgian fort.

Below: DFS 230 gliders towed by Ju 52s would be used for the attack on the fort.

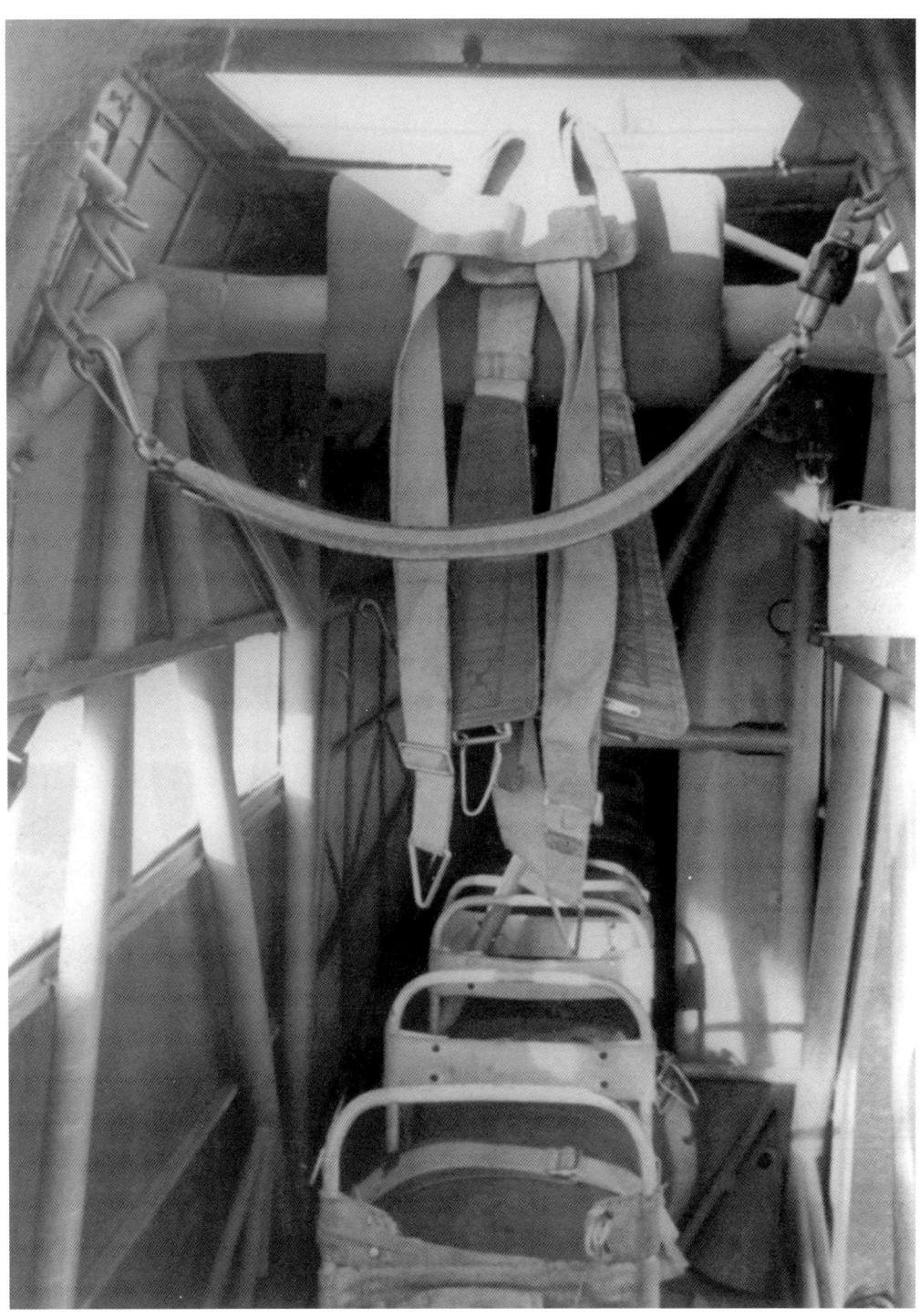

The narrow interior of one of the combat gliders. It could carry ten men, including the pilot, who, once on the ground, fought alongside his comrades.

A photograph of Eben-Emael Fort taken in April by a reconnaissance aircraft. Note that the banks (glacis) of the fort are devoid of any defences (either weapons or obstacles).

The DFS 230s, painted in white and devoid of markings, after landing on the glacis.

Although blurred, this is an important photograph as it shows the meeting of the land forces with Hauptmann Walter Koch (bandaged head), who led the 'Concrete Group' which captured Eben-Emael.

Above: The capture of the fort would not be without sacrifices. Here, two *Fallschirmjäger* tombs have been dug in haste on the glacis.

Below: After the surrender of the fort and the arrival of the ground troops, the paratroopers gathered together in the village of Eben-Emael.

Following the fighting, airmen examine one of Eben-Emael's casemates that has been destroyed by a hollow charge carried by the paratroopers.

The bodies of paratroopers killed at Eben-Emael would later be collected.

On 15 May 1940, Adolf Hitler met with those *Fallschirmjäger* who had distinguished themselves during the fighting on the Albert Canal. L to R: *Leutnant* Egon Delica, *Oberleutnant* Rudolf Witzig, *Hauptmann* Walter Koch, *Oberleutnant* Otto Zierach, Adolf Hitler, *Leutnant* Helmut Ringler, *Leutnant* Joachim Meissner, *Oberleutnant* and glider commander Walter Kiess, *Oberleutnant* Gustav Altmann and Dr Rolf Jäger.

Other paratroopers would be honoured with the *Ritterkreuz*, including *Feldwebel* Helmut Arpke, a member of the 'Concrete Group', who received the decoration on 13 May 1940. He is immortalised here on a poster by the famous propaganda artist Wolf Willrich. Arpke would fight in Crete, but was killed on 16 January 1942 in Charkowa (USSR).

Above: 10 May 1940, the great mass of the airborne head off towards the Netherlands.

Below: Paratroopers board their aircraft. Their destination was Rotterdam or the various bridges deemed essential for the German advance.

Above: A mass jump over the Netherlands.

Below: The first prisoners captured from the Dutch army.

A paratrooper stands guard at one end of the captured, and still intact, Dordrecht bridge.

The Moerdijk bridge was also one of the airborne's main objectives. The white dots on this aerial photograph are abandoned parachutes.

A small monument erected after the fighting in Moerdijk to honour the airborne who were killed during the operation.

A container drop.

Above: Two paratroopers in charge of a mortar.

Below: Specialised units and reinforcements arrive in the Netherlands by road with the other regular units.

Although the Führer met with some of the Eben-Emael fighters at his headquarters, his air marshal (Hermann Göring) personally handed over various decorations to the paratroopers deployed in the Netherlands. He is seen here on 24 May with *Oberst* Bruno Bräuer. On Bräuer's left are *Hauptmann* Fritz Prager and *Oberleutnant* Horst Kerfin. All three were awarded the *Ritterkreuz*.

A group of paratroopers after the fighting.

Chapter 3

July 1940-April 1941: Reorganization and Resumption of Fighting

Once France had surrendered on 21 June 1940, only Great Britain remained. But the British government, which was the first to declare war on the Reich, had no intention of following the example of its unfortunate ally and, on the contrary, gave the order to attack the French fleet at Mers-el-Kébir, thus sending a very clear message to Berlin.

It seemed that as early as 18 June 1940, Air Marshal Ehrard Milch had the idea of repeating the tactics of the Netherlands campaign: drop all available paratroopers in the south-east of England and occupy the various aerodromes in the region. This meant that Ju 52 carriers, Bf 109 fighters and Ju 87 dive bombers could then be established on English soil while reinforcements would be transported by sea. Milch understood that if you wanted to invade the British Isles, you needed to act quickly (it is worth noting, however, that unlike the Luftwaffe, the RAF had hardly been affected by the fighting on the continent and could have therefore have countered such an aerial invasion). Aware of Hitler's hesitancy, the British government procrastinated and made various proposals without taking any further action. The *Fallschirmjäger* consequently returned to their barracks to reorganize because, although the May 1940 campaign had been a success, it also revealed a number of deficiencies. The *22.Infanteriedivision* would receive the honorific nickname "*Luftlande*" (airborne), but would never be used again. In return, the *Fallschirmjäger* increased its efficiency after certain secondary units were reinforced, while two new regiments were created. Following the expansion of the airborne troops, they were now grouped in the new *XI.Fliegerkorps*.

To keep the men occupied, exercises with combat gliders took place as part of Operation *Seelöwe* (sea lion), the planned invasion of Great Britain. However, this would only be a whiff of propaganda. In fact, on 12 October 1940, Operation *Seelöwe* was postponed indefinitely and its abandonment was later followed on 11 December 1941 by another cancellation, that of *Unternehmen Felix*, which involved the capture of Gibraltar, an operation which would certainly have required the use of airborne forces. The paratroopers then enjoyed a long period of calm, which would break down partially in late February 1941, when part of the FJR 2 was sent to the Balkans. The Italian-Greek war turned out very badly for the troops of Benito Mussolini and the British, Greece's ally, risked taking advantage of this opportunity to set foot on the continent and threaten the Romanian oil fields which were essential to the *Wehrmacht*. Germany had to intervene. Hearing about the Italian invasion of Greece in October 1940, Hitler had rushed to Milan to offer *il Duce* the loan of airborne troops in order to capture the island of Crete, which acted as a kind of "natural aircraft carrier" in the eastern Mediterranean. But the Führer arrived far too late and could only watch as a spectator as the evolving situation turned into a disaster for his transalpine ally. In 1941, the *Fallschirmjäger* would operate well in south-eastern Europe.

When Operation *Marita* (the invasion of Yugoslavia and mainland Greece) began on 6 April 1941, paratroopers were put on the alert. The campaign went very well for the German armies and on 25 April the troops left Bulgaria (where they were stationed) to fly to the Greek airfield of Larissa, which had recently been captured. Ju 52s and DFS 230 gliders were posted there and the order arrived the following day to engage several sections in the Corinth sector. The objective was the bridge crossing the famous canal that separated the Peloponnese from the rest of mainland Greece. Landing near the British positions (either gliding or having been dropped by the Ju 52s), the *Fallschirmjäger* captured a number of Commonwealth soldiers, but could not prevent the destruction of the bridge. However, their intervention has prevented many enemy units from retreating and several prisoners were taken. On 28 April the airborne saw the arrival of the mountain troops. The cost of the operation for the FJR 2 was sixty-three dead and sixteen missing (those paratroopers who were seen on the bridge shortly before its destruction).

Above: Back in their barracks, the *Fallschirmjäger* resumed their training for a possible attack on England.

Below: In the plans for Operation Seelöwe (the invasion of England), DFS 230s would be used and the drops should follow one after the other

Above: A DFS 230 lands during training for Operation Seelöwe.

Below: Parachutists set up a heavy machine gun, under the watchful eyes of children who are carefully watching this exciting exercise.

Above: Jumping from a Ju 52.

Below: Although England would not be their next objective, the *Fallschirmjäger* would nevertheless be quickly deployed under other skies.

Training makes you hungry.

Chapter 4

May 1941: The Battle of Crete (Operation *Merkur*)

Despite the success of Operation *Marita* [the German invasion of Greece], Crete was still held by a British-Greek garrison, additionally reinforced by many soldiers who had been able to evacuate mainland Greece. After a final call for peace offered by the Führer was rejected, the order was given to conquer this last British stronghold.

Paratroopers would be required, given the distance, although this time they would not constitute a support force, but rather the spearhead of the *Wehrmacht*. At the end of April, the entire *7.Fliegerdivision*, as well as elements of *XI. Fl.K.* had reached Athens, primarily using the network of bumpy Balkan roads which had been further damaged by the war. Equipment stored in France in anticipation of Operation *Seelöwe* now had to be sent to Greece. For several days, the *Fallschirmjäger* assembled in Attica awaiting orders and on 19 May they gathered together to be told that Operation *Merkur* would begin the following day.

The paratroopers divided into three groups and were transported by Ju 52s to three main areas on the northern coast of the island: to the east, the capital Chania (with the important harbour in Souda Bay and the excellent airfield at Maleme); in the centre, Rethymnon (with a very basic aerodrome) and, in the east, the large city of Heraklion (with a good aerodrome). The *Fallschirmjäger* needed to take control of these aerodromes, as well as sections of the coast, to allow the delivery of reinforcements and supplies both by air and sea (two convoys of small fishing boats loaded with mountain troops had to land in Crete on the night of 20-21 May). The plan was simple and should have succeeded.

But, in a dramatic twist for the German forces, the invaders were expected. Although it would be another forty years before this knowledge came to light, Luftwaffe messages sent via the Enigma machine had been intercepted and the defenders knew all the details of the enemy's plan, including the precise locations of the drops. This meant that during the night of 19-20 May, Commonwealth troops began positioning themselves around the landing zones.

On 20 May, three assault waves crossed the Aegean Sea. There were a few accidents and, to further complicate the airborne's task, General Wilhelm Süssmann, who was in charge of coordinating the entire operation, was killed shortly after take off when his DFS 230 crashed. He was quickly replaced by *Oberst* Richard Heidrich who, unfortunately, was not fully briefed on the operation.

Arriving on the island of Crete, the Ju 52 formations came under fire from the few anti-aircraft guns that were available to the Allies. Although many of the aircraft were hit, their passengers were still able jump, but the paratroopers then became easy targets as they descended towards the earth and consequently suffered particularly high casualty rates. However, as soon as the survivors touched the ground, the *Fallschirmjäger*'s exceptional training came to the fore. NCOs replaced those officers who had disappeared and took control of small detachments. They also benefited from the steep terrain, which helped them in hand-to-hand combat situations. On the opposite side, the Allies had little means of communication and were consequently not as mobile as their opponents.

However, the situation was almost hopeless for paratroopers, especially since the two rescue fleets were quickly made to retreat by the Royal Navy. The German command now had to risk everything, sacrificing the two groups in the east and centre and moving the main arm of the offensive towards the western end of the island, where reinforcements also sent. The mountain troops returned to their ports and were then transported by Ju 52s to Maleme aerodrome as soon as it was captured.

Despite the bloody fighting, the airborne troops were able to take up positions near Chania, before moving east to join the small groups of men who were still engaged in a fierce battle with Commonwealth soldiers.

When the fate of the armies began to turn, the Allies very often resorted to desperate tactics. On several occasions, Australian or New Zealand soldiers (ANZACS) appealed to the local population for help by falsely claiming that German paratroopers (although in the minority) would not take prisoners. By galvanising the Cretans (who were often armed to the teeth), the Allies broke all laws of war and many paratroopers were massacred by civilians.

On 1 June, after the final Allied soldiers had been evacuated to Egypt, Operation *Merkur* could be considered completed: Crete was finally conquered. However, the price paid by the Germans was terrifying: out of 8,000 *Fallschirmjäger*, around 4,000 were killed - half of the parachute force - while the other half who survived were wounded to varying degrees. The surprisingly high percentage of those registered missing is explained by the actions of the islanders. In the following years, the German occupying forces would regularly find the bodies of paratroopers that had been mutilated and secretly buried during the fighting of May 1941. Hence the inevitable reprisals that, until now, have fuelled many of the official Cretan historiographies which, of course, overlook the war crimes that were knowingly committed by these same civilians.

The damage to resources was also serious. In the flights over Crete, or during the support operations at Maleme, 136 of the 500 Ju 52s were destroyed and many more were damaged. These losses, added to those suffered during the invasion of The Netherlands just a year earlier, had weakened German aerial transportation, right on the eve of another important operation: the invasion of the USSR.

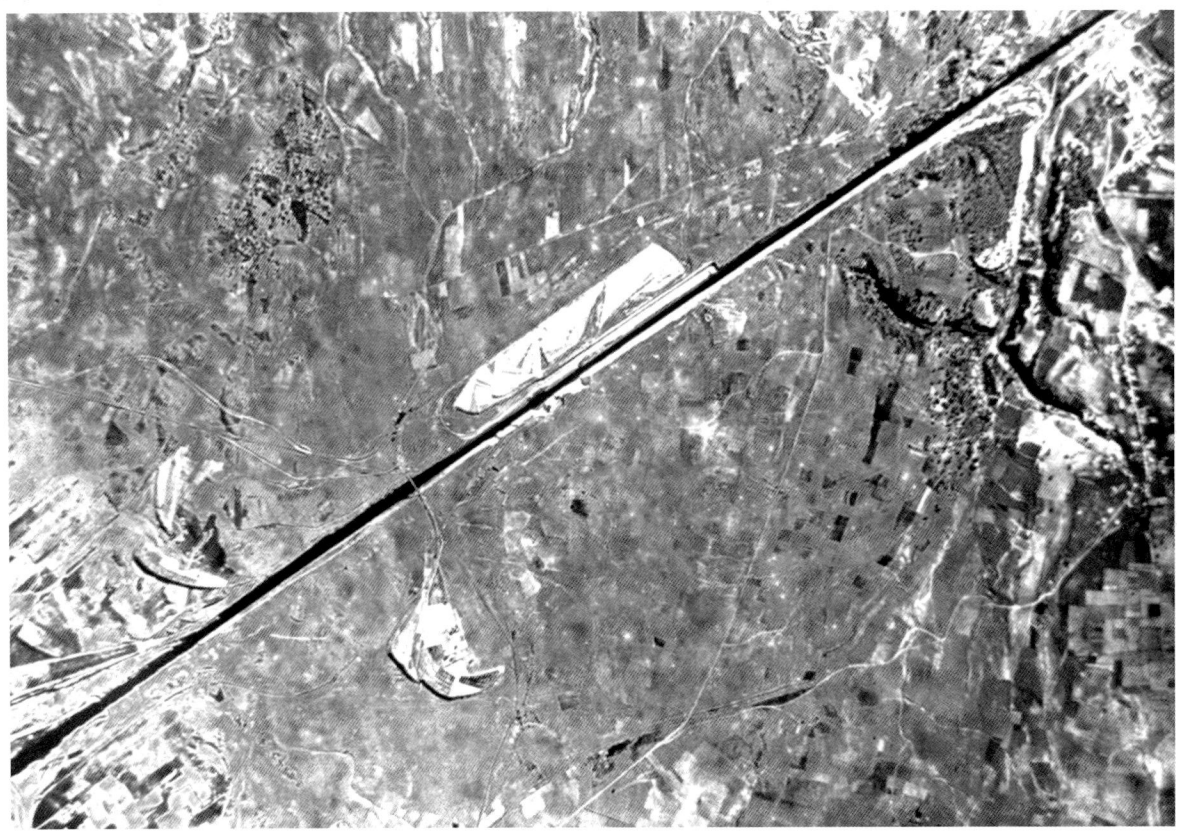

The Corinth Canal photographed by a reconnaissance aircraft. There were hardly any strategic bridges spanning the gap.

Above: Larissa Aerodrome, 25 April 1941. Ju 52s and DFS 230 are assembled ready for the attack the next day.

Below: On April 26, 1941, the *Fallschirmjäger* set off for Corinth.

Above: The bridge over the canal was destroyed while several paratroopers were crossing it. A German war correspondent, who was also an artist, gave his personal interpretation of this murderous episode.

Opposite above: The surrounding area soon fell into German hands. The city's mayor surrendered in front of *Oberst* Alfred Sturm, the commander of FJR 2.

Opposite below: The attack was not completed without losses, as shown by this wreck of a DFS 230 glider.

A small cemetery constructed near the canal.

A pontoon was built over the canal to replace the bridge. Despite the destruction of the bridge, the airborne managed to cut off the retreat for many Commonwealth soldiers.

Leutnant Wilhelm Fulda (seen here on one of Wolf Willrich's postcards), commanded 3./LLG 1, a combat glider unit attached to 6./FJR2. He was awarded the Knight's Cross for his participation in the assault on Corinth. His life and military career were very rich: born in 1909 in Antwerp (Belgium), he was a specialist in combat gliders at the beginning of the Second World War. At the end of 1942, he led a unit of Go 242 heavy gliders before training as a fighter pilot and commanding several single-engine night fighter groups. In 1945, he was head of the 1./JG 400, a unit equipped with Me 163 rocket fighters. Wilhelm Fulda died in 1977, in Hamburg.

Paratrooper reinforcements were initially sent to the Balkans by train to take part in the invasion of Crete.

They were also transported by road. On this occasion, the Germans have discovered the rough nature of the local roads, which led to several punctures.

The men played checkers to kill time....

... but also carefully prepared the containers that would be dropped with them on Crete.

After arriving in Athens, paratroopers had the opportunity to tour the Greek capital. For some some of them, this would be their last chance for relaxation.

The interior of one of the containers. Hand grenades were particularly popular.

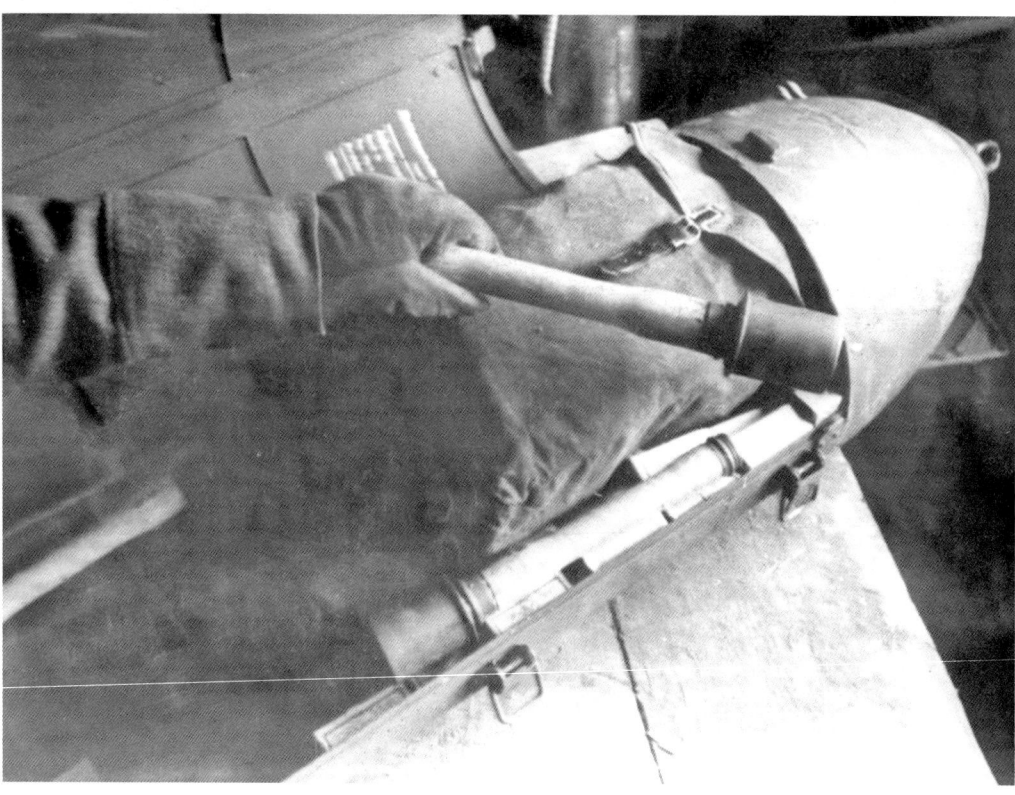

After collecting their life jackets, needed in case of a crash, they climb into the plane.

Above: 20 May 1941. The paratroopers prepare for boarding, under the watchful eyes of a Ju 52 crew member.

Below: Taking off for Crete from Topolia airfield (Attica).

The large dust clouds released during take-offs and landings strongly hindered the speed of the shuttles. Due to fears of collisions or accidents, the clouds had to settle first and delays would naturally ensue, which were obviously damaging to the smooth running of Operation *Merkur*.

"*Unter uns, Kreta*". Below us, Crete.

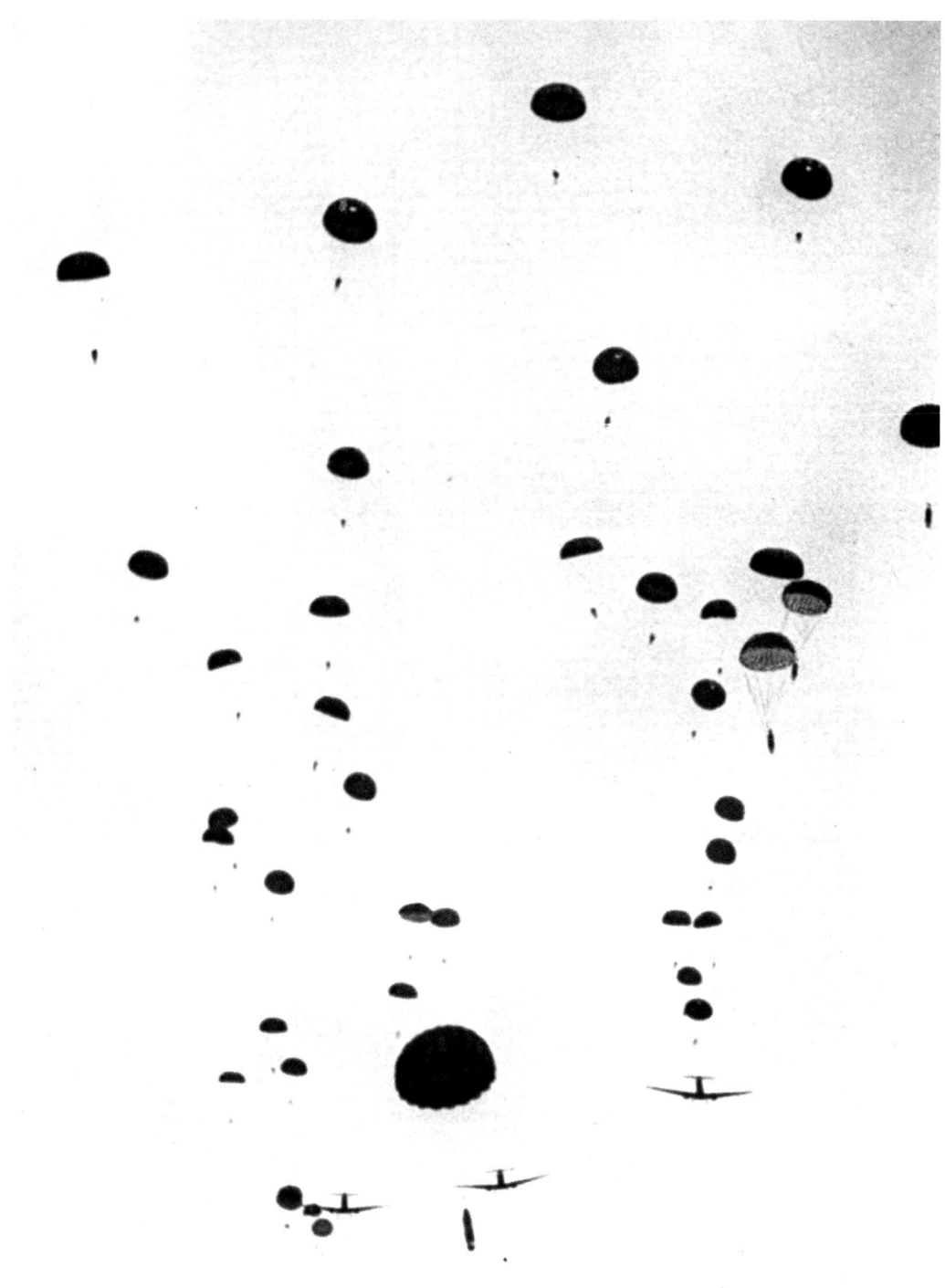

The drop on the three fixed objectives was massive. But on the ground, well aware of the enemy's plan, the defenders were waiting.

A Ju 52 loaded with *Fallschirmjäger* on its way to Crete.

During their descent, the defenceless *Fallschirmjäger* were a very easy target for the shooters on the ground.

Although some experts say that this famous photograph of Souda Bay has been doctored, it does give a good idea of the events of 20 May, including the sight of a Ju 52 plunging to the sea whilst on fire. The losses among the aircraft would be very high.

DFS 230 pilots sometimes had to land their glider close to enemy positions. If the occupants were able to exit quickly enough then they were likely to neutralise their opponent. Otherwise, they risked being hit by grape shot.

An MG 34 machine gun positioned at the front of the DFS 230 provided little defensive protection on landing.

A Ju 52 flies over a portion of the Cretan coast. Once again, the white dots are parachutes spread out on the ground, but this time they are often covering the corpse of a dead paratrooper.

Den Heldentod
fürs Vaterland starb
Feldwebel
Josef Brunner
Fallschirm-Jäger
geboren am 22. Dezember 1917
gefallen am 20. Mai 1941
auf Kreta

Er zog von uns mit stolzem Herzen
und hoffte auf ein Wiederseh'n,
doch groß sind jetzt nun uns're
Schmerzen,
da dieses nicht mehr kann gescheh'n;
so schlafe wohl in fremder Erden,
von uns wirst nie vergessen werden.

R. I. P.

Süßes Herz Mariä, sei meine
Rettung!
Süßes Herz Jesu, sei meine
Liebe!
Vater unser. — Ave Maria.

Faced with this deluge of fire, the *Fallschirmjäger* had to dig defensive positions and often fought side by side. Many officers had either been killed or wounded and each paratrooper had to have confidence in his own excellent training and survival instincts.

A death notice for one of the many paratroopers killed on the first day of Operation *Merkur*.

All the local command in Athens could do was to send fighters and Ju 87 *Stukas* to strafe and bomb the Allied batteries. These paratroopers are biding their time by waiting in a trench.

Despite their heavy losses, the *Fallschirmjäger* were soon able to counter-attack.

They were even able to take prisoners.

Meanwhile, further waves of paratroopers were sent in as reinforcements.

A speedy departure. Time was running out to save their comrades who were desperately struggling across the Aegean Sea.

After capturing the Maleme airfield, Ju 52s loaded with mountain troops were now able to land. However, the Allies were able to attack the runway and many aeroplanes were destroyed.

Above: A mountain fighter rather sluggishly leaves the runway at Maleme, after recovering his combat equipment from his burning Ju 52.

Below: The situation gradually turned to the invaders' advantage and the *Fallschirmjäger* were able to leave their defensive positions.

New prisoners were taken.

An NCO paratrooper observes the enemy's positions.

Many war correspondents in Crete would fall in battle. To compensate for the lack of photographic material, *Der Adler* published beautiful drawings of the various actions.

A captured British Bofors (anti-aircraft) gun is used against its previous owners.

A wounded paratrooper.

Mountain troops have joined the paratroopers and are jointly guiding the artillery fire.

Generalmajor Eugen Meindl, commander of the *Sturmregiment*, in a heroic pose typical of the artist Wolf Willrich (this portrait would be exhibited in 1942). Meindl was wounded on the first day of the Battle of Crete, and was evacuated from the island by Ju 52 thanks to a brave crew. Command of the regiment was then swiftly taken over by one of his subordinates, Major Edgar Stentzler.

Gradually, the paratroopers demonstrated their qualities and conquered the island with the support of mountain troops.

A moment of relaxation in the courtyard of an islander's house. Despite the Cretan 'resistance' propaganda developed after the war, the entire population of the island did not take part in the fighting.

Taking advantage of the motorbikes dropped by the Ju 52s, the invaders were able to move more efficiently along the coastal road that connected the island's three main cities.

A group of paratroopers taking a short break before entering Chania. The Cretan capital fell on 27 May after a week of fierce fighting.

After the fighting, *Oberst* Bernhard Ramcke gives a speech to some of the survivors from the *Sturmregiment*.

Crete was finally conquered on 1 June 1941, after the last of the Allies had evacuated the island, and now the *Landser* [a German colloquial term for an army soldier] could carry out an inventory of the damage. These paratroopers are posing on the wreckage of one of the 130 Ju 52s that were destroyed during Operation *Merkur*.

Now was the time for justice and punishments. During the occupation of the island, corpses of paratroopers who had been mutilated or massacred by islanders were often found. Investigations took place and paratroopers would regularly have the unpleasant duty of forming platoons to shoot those Cretans who were guilty of such actions (on the other hand, Allied soldiers who incited them to commit these crimes had nothing to worry about).

Above: The paratroopers lost 4,000 men. Even if a large number of the corpses were never found (fallen at sea or hidden by the islanders), the graves would still cover a large portion of the island.

Below: The tomb of a DFS 230 pilot (note the glider's canopy) and some of his passengers.

A war correspondent captured this famous image of a mountain trooper (note the edelweiss on his sleeve) at the grave of a paratrooper; probably a brother, cousin or childhood friend.

Paratroopers being brought back to Attica by boat contemplate the wreckages of ships that were still on fire in Souda Bay.

Above: The return to the barracks in Germany was meant to be victorious, but the faces are serious due to the heavy losses.

Below: The survivors on a victory parade, but their ranks were severely depleted. These paratroopers have returned to Tangermünde from Crete with a mascot: a baby donkey.

Official parades took place in garrison towns.

In mid-June, Kurt Student visited his paratroopers who had remained in Crete. He is greeted here (most likely at Maleme) by a general (note the stripes on his trousers) who must be the newest commander in Crete, *General* Alexander Andrae, the former commander of the *Luftgau Balkan*.

Student and Andrae leave the airfield with a paratrooper guiding the two generals. On the right is *General* Ferdinand Schörner, commander of *6.Gebirgsdivision*, whose mountain troops were still garrisoned on the island. Note that Andrae, like Student, is wearing the badge of former members of the Imperial Air Force. Schörner was also a veteran of the Great War and had been awarded the *Pour le Mérite* military order.

Alongside *Major* Karl-Lothar Schulz (left) and his superior Bräuer, *General* Student examines one of the few British Mathilda tanks used by the defenders of Crete. The appearance of these armoured vehicles had been a big surprise for aircrafts, which often had no anti-tank weaponry. The bearded officer on the right with a tropical helmet would appear to be *Major* Julius Ringel, the famous commander of *5.Gebirgsdivision* ('*Die Gams*').

It goes without saying that the general took advantage of his visit to decorate several deserving soldiers.

Many Knight's Crosses were awarded following the astonishing success of Operation *Merkur*, in spite of the terrible odds. Major Ludwig Heilman, commander of III./FJR 3, was one of the recipients. Born in 1903, he joined the *Reichswehr* and began the Second World War in an infantry regiment. Fascinated by the exploits of the airborne, in the mid-1940s he volunteered for the *Fallschirmjäger* and ended the war as a *Generalmajor*. He died in 1959.

Another recipient of the *Ritterkreuz* on 14 June 1941 was *Oberleutnant* Gerhard Schirmer. Born in 1913, he was one of those policemen who had retrained as a paratrooper. Having fought in the Netherlands and Corinth, this company commander from FJR 2 distinguished himself at Heraklion. Schirmer survived the war and ended his military career in the new *Bundeswehr*.

MEINDL, GÉNÉRAL-MAJOR

HEIDRICH, COLONEL

STURM, COLONEL

STENTZLER, MAJOR

HEILMANN, MAJOR

BARON V. D. HEYDTE, CAPITAINE

Der Adler magazine naturally published the photographs of the men who had been awarded the Ritterkreuz in Crete. Here are some recipients from 14 June 1941: *Generalmajor* Eugen Meindl (injured 20 May 1941), *Oberst* Richard Heidrich (commander of FJR 3), *Oberst* Alfred Sturm (FJR 2), Major Edgar Stentzler (II./*Sturmregiment*), *Major* Ludwig Heilmann (III./FJR 3) and *Hauptmann* Friedrich-August (baron) von der Heydte (I./FJR 3).

Above: Those Junkers 52s which were damaged but repairable were dismantled and brought back to the mainland. Crete was also expensive in terms of transportation resources and the Luftwaffe suffered heavy losses there from which it would struggle to recover.

Below: Some parachutists remained in the garrison on Crete and had time to examine captured British equipment, such as this Bren Carrier.

After recuperating and establishing positions on Crete before the arrival of the army and German administration, the *Fallschirmjäger* left for the continent. *Major* Edgar Stentzler and his men left in a Ju 52 with a new mascot for the II./ *Sturmregiment*: a Cretan donkey. A few weeks later, Stentzler was killed in the USSR.

The detachments that remained behind built cemeteries for the many soldiers who were killed during Operation *Merkur*. This image shows the monument at the *Heldenfriedhof* (Heroes' Cemetery) in Heraklion. The sculptor has perfectly reproduced the *Fallschirmjäger* emblem.

In contrast, the monument erected in Aptera (near Chania) in honour of the men from the *Sturmregiment* was preserved (although the swastika held in the eagle's claws would be removed). This image was taken in 1973, before various construction works had completely invaded the area.

The plaque is still in place on the Aptera monument.

The completed monument would be destroyed after 1945 and the graves transferred to Maleme's large military cemetery, overlooking the airfield that cost the lives of so many soldiers on both sides.

Chapter 5

September 1941: The USSR (Operation *Barbarossa*)

On 22 June 1941, Germany launched its assault on the Soviet giant in a campaign that everyone believed would be very short.

The losses suffered during the Crete campaign (both in men and equipment) had naturally scared the German high command, who now had little regard for the future of the airborne. As Kurt Student said: "Crete was the tomb of the German paratrooper". Pending the reorganisation of their hard-hit units, the *Fallschirmjäger*, who had just returned from the Mediterranean, were now urgently deployed on the new Eastern Front to fill in the gaps.

The first shipment to the USSR took place in September 1941, when Major Edgar Stentzler's second battalion was flown by Ju 52s from Goslar to Petruschino to destroy the Soviet bridgehead there. The strong point was indeed destroyed, but at the cost of heavy casualties in both camps. Stentzler, one of the heroes of the Battle of Crete, was among the dead.

Gradually, other battalions were routed to the Leningrad sector to reinforce those units of the *Heer* that had been assigned to other tasks. Under the command of *Generalmajor* Erich Petersen, the paratroopers would fight for more than a month and repel some 140 enemy assaults. During the fighting, they destroyed 40 tanks, took 3,400 prisoners and would even be credited with shooting down 5 Soviet aircraft shot down using their machine guns and light weapons. However, this was all at the cost of 3,000 killed or wounded paratroopers.

The northern sector would not be the only one to see *Fallschirmjäger* fight as elite infantrymen. Alongside other specialised companies, the 2nd Regiment would be deployed on the Mius Front, while the first battalion of the *Sturmregiment* (which was largely illustrated in Crete) would fight on the Moscow Front.

It could be suggested that by the end of 1941, the *Fallschirmjäger*'s fate had been sealed and that as a weapon, it would simply blend into the mass of the *Heer*.

However, the year 1942 would experience a revival of the German paratrooper which, like the phoenix, would be reborn from the ashes. Nevertheless, it would never again reach the same heights as its earlier exploits.

The paratroopers had experienced victory in May 1941, but at a great cost, and now several of its members would take part in the first battles in the USSR, alongside the infantrymen. Here, a paratrooper is in position on the Leningrad Front.

Despite this new deployment to the USSR, the *Fallschirmjäger* remained elite fighters thanks to their excellent training and morale.

However, the list of the dead would also grow longer in the USSR as well. Among them were many veterans of Crete or the fighting in May 1940.

Snipers on the Leningrad Front.

The arrival of snow would hinder operations.

The paratroopers had to adapt to the conditions and the snow reminded them of the Scandinavian countryside from the previous year. However, temperatures in the USSR would drop very quickly and very severely.

In front of an *izba* (traditional Russian log cabin).

On patrol in front of
Soviet lines.

Paratroopers
sometimes had to
turn into skiers.